SIMPLE GUIDE TO
INDONESIA
CUSTOMS AND ETIQUETTE

ILLUSTRATED BY
IRENE SANDERSON

SIMPLE GUIDE TO

INDONESIA

CUSTOMS & ETIQUETTE

GRAHAM SAUNDERS

GLOBAL BOOKS LTD

Simple Guides • Series 1
CUSTOMS & ETIQUETTE

The Simple Guide to
INDONESIA
CUSTOMS & ETIQUETTE
by Graham Saunders

First Published 2001 by

GLOBAL BOOKS LTD
PO Box 219, Folkestone, Kent, England CT20 3LZ

ISBN 1-86034-016-4

British Library Cataloguing in Publication Data
A CIP catalogue entry for this book
is available from the British Library

Set in Futura 11 on 12pt by Mark Heslington, Scarborough,
North Yorkshire
Printed in Malta by Interprint Ltd

Contents

Foreword

Carved mask

Indonesia is a vast country of great diversity. Comprising over 13,000 islands, it stretches for more than 5000 kilometres from the northern tip of Sumatra to Irian Jaya in New Guinea. Its 200 million inhabitants speak over 500 languages and dialects, reflecting its cultural and ethnic diversity. Predominantly Muslim, it has large Hindu, Buddhist, Christian and Animist minorities. The population is unevenly spread. Java, only the fifth largest island, boasts almost half the total.

Indonesia is the giant of Southeast Asia not only in terms of size and population. Strategically located between the Pacific and Indian Oceans, it has enormous economic potential and is a major regional power. Its diversity presents any government with its major challenge, and from the

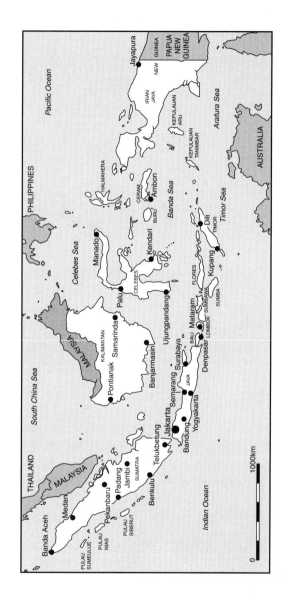

Map of Indonesia

creation of the unitary republic in 1950, the motto inscribed on the national coat of arms has been 'Bhinneka Tunggal Ika', meaning 'They are many: they are one' – 'Unity in Diversity'.

The words are Sanskrit, the language of Hindu scripture. Indonesia is the largest Muslim country in the world, but Islam rests on Hindu and Animist foundations long predating its arrival. The red and white Indonesian flag bears the colours of the pre-Islamic Javanese kingdom of Majapahit. Popular culture is imbued with the stories, themes and characters of the great Hindu epics, the *Ramayana* and the *Mahabharata*. Hinduism remains the religion of the island of Bali.

Religion is of great significance in the life of the most 'modern' of Indonesians. Islam established itself firmly in the fifteenth century. Buddhism is exemplified in the great ninth-century monument of Borobudur in Central Java, and is now mainly practised by urban Indonesians of Chinese descent. Christianity arrived in its Catholic manifestation with the Portuguese in the sixteenth century and in its Protestant form with the Dutch in the seventeenth. It retains strongholds in the outer islands, like Ambon and Timor, and has many adherents throughout. Animism remains prevalent in Borneo and Irian Jaya, although under pressure from both Islam and Christianity.

Whatever their form of worship, Indonesians possess a strong religious sense. Belief in God is the first of the *Pantja Sila*, or Five Principles, which define the state (the others are *Sovereignty of the People*, *Nationalism*, *Social Justice* and *Internationalism*).

Religion permeates the lives of Indonesians to an extent no longer true in the West. Custom, behaviour and etiquette are based upon religious concepts which define an individual's status, role and worth. But these attitudes and beliefs are not drawn from one single source. Over the centuries Indonesians have blended the various influences that have impacted upon them, including many acquired from Europe. They have not done so to a uniform extent, however, so that there are variations in what is considered acceptable in different parts of Indonesia.

Jakarta itself, a cultural melting pot, is a special case. Even Indonesians may speak of it as a separate entity. However, just as there is a common language in Bahasa Indonesia, which is understood throughout the country, so there is a general code of behaviour which is acceptable in most areas and most situations.

This book is designed to help you understand how to do the right things and avoid giving offence. It provides a guide to general behaviour, but also helps you to understand the values and principles which underlie the customs and etiquette of Indonesian society.

Indonesia has passed through a difficult time since 1997. Visitors should not be deterred. Given its size and diversity, many regions have been largely unaffected and a welcome still awaits you. The country has had crises before and recovered. The sensible tourist and business traveller will check on the situation in any places he or she wishes to visit and plan accordingly.

GRAHAM SAUNDERS

1

A Brief History

Traditional Karo Batak house

Human habitation dates back some 500,000 years to Java Man. Migration into the region and to Australia was across the land bridge from Asia to Australia created by lower sea levels during the Ice Ages. To this day, the islands rest on the now submerged Sunda shelf and the seas are relatively shallow.

By the beginning of the Christian era, trading kingdoms had arisen and Hinduism and, later, Buddhism arrived in a process historians call Indianization. The remains of Hindu and Buddhist temples which are prevalent, particularly in central

Java, testify to the wealth and power of these kingdoms, while Hinduism survives as a living faith on Bali.

The kingdom of Srivijaya on Sumatra controlled for several centuries the sea trade of the region. It was superseded in the fourteenth century by the Javanese empire of Majapahit, the extent and glory of which permeate the Javanese consciousness to the present day.

Islam arrived in the archipelago conveyed by Arab and, later, Indian and Chinese Muslim traders. It had gained a firm foothold in northern Sumatra by the end of the thirteenth century and in Java in the fifteenth. In the sixteenth century the Portuguese, seeking spices, established trading posts in the Moluccas and eventually expelled their rivals, the Spanish. In the seventeenth century, the Dutch established themselves in Batavia (now Jakarta), excluded their English rivals and confined the Portuguese to East Timor. By the end of the nineteenth century, the Dutch had established their control over all of what was called the Dutch East Indies.

In the early years of the twentieth century, a nationalist movement emerged, which developed three main forms: Islamic, with its stress upon Muslim culture and Islamic law; Communist, seeking social revolution and the restructuring of society; and secular nationalism aiming at the creation of an independent Indonesian state. These were not entirely exclusive and disparate movements. No nationalist movement could ignore Islam, social and economic inequalities and the presence of the Dutch. The colonial regime made some concessions, but suppressed the nationalist movement and imprisoned or exiled its leaders.

The victorious Japanese released leaders like Ahmad Sukarno and Mahomed Hatta in 1942 and sought their collaboration. The Communists could expect no mercy from the Japanese and went underground. Sukarno and his supporters pursued the nationalist agenda within the restrictions imposed by the Japanese authorities. These were relaxed from 1943 on as the war turned against the Japanese and they began to groom Indonesians as potential allies.

Sukarno skilfully used his position to establish his credentials as the nationalist leader and on 17 August 1945, declared Indonesia's independence with himself as President. After a bitter war, the Dutch recognized the new Republic in 1949, although it was not until 1962 that they withdrew from what is now the province of Irian Jaya.

Indonesia has had a chequered history since independence. Under President Sukarno it was a leader within the non-aligned movement of the 1950s, but economic development was uneven. Sukarno was a charismatic and popular leader, who maintained a precarious balance between the Muslims, the Communists and the Army, the latter acquiring political importance as the defenders of the Republic. The political crisis of the mid-1960s saw General Suharto come to power and preside over three decades of rapid economic growth. However, political power lay with an elite which became corrupt, autocratic, self-seeking and out of touch with the people, leading to economic crisis and the overthrow of Suharto in 1998.

Hot Tip: A Friendly & Hospitable People

Despite recent economic and political events, Indonesia has great potential which will lead to eventual recovery. The violence which flared was localized. Indonesia is a vast country and remains safe to visit. The foreign visitor is welcomed and will find the country one of great variety, spectacular natural scenery, fascinating cultural treasures and friendly and hospitable people.

HISTORICAL SITES

Wherever you visit there is likely to be much of historical interest, but the richest concentration of sites is found on Java. In central Java, near Yogyakarta, are the remains of the historic Hindu and Buddhist kingdoms, including the famous Borobudur, over 1,000 years old and the world's largest Buddhist monument, and the magnificent Hindu temples of Prambanan. The Muslim rulers of Yogyakarta and its nearby rival Surakarta (also known as 'Solo') retained much of the traditional ceremony and culture so that both cities are repositories of Javanese music, dance, art and crafts.

If you are restricted by time and opportunity to Jakarta, the National Museum in Jakarta's Medan Merdeka (Freedom Square) houses a fine collection of Indonesian antiquities. The square itself offers fine examples of Dutch colonial architecture, including the Presidential Palace; while the huge Istiqlal Mosque and the 137 metre high marble National Monument in the centre of the square celebrate Islam and independence.

As 'Batavia', Jakarta was the capital of the Dutch colonial regime and a visit to Taman Fatahillah in the old colonial area known as Kota provides the best insight to the Dutch period. Housed in the old Dutch Stadhuis or city hall is the Jakarta City Museum, with its collection of Dutch colonial memorabilia, as well as material from earlier times.

Also worth visiting are the Wayang Museum, devoted to the traditional puppet theatre, and the Balai Seni Rupa art gallery which displays modern Indonesian art and collections of Chinese porcelain and Javanese terra cottas from the Majapahit period.

Wherever you go in Indonesia, look out for examples of this rich past. In some areas, there may be little physical evidence of the pre-Muslim era or of the colonial. In others, remnants are preserved in local museums, or may be sitting almost neglected on the side of the road. In Bali, Hinduism in its Balinese form remains a living culture.

Meanwhile, the Indonesian carries within him a legacy of this rich past. Down-town Jakarta may boast a skyline as ultra-modern as any in the world, but its inhabitants reflect in their beliefs, behaviour and culture elements from many layers of their historic past. And this is as true of the inhabitants of Bali as of Aceh. What is remarkable is how out of such ethnic, cultural and historical disparity, an Indonesian nation has been created.

Nusa Dua beach

2

Social & Community Values

Traditional wedding 'bersanding'

Indonesians of all ethnic groups value the family and the community, though this may appear less evident among the younger generation and the urban population most affected by modernization and increasing physical and social mobility. Even so, the more recent arrivals to the cities attempt to retain contact with their families and home villages.

Indonesians are generous people and even the poorest will press some small gift upon a visitor. It is best to reciprocate in kind, with some small item.

Something from your own country is appreciated as are sweets and small gifts for the children.

STRENGTH OF THE FAMILY

Indonesians are family-orientated and children are valued, petted and indulged. Very early in an acquaintance expect to be asked politely about your own family, especially whether you have children. Indonesian friends may ask questions a Westerner considers intrusive. This is not from impoliteness, and you may ask similar questions.

Indonesians seek to establish a person's place in the general order of things, so your occupation, family status and pattern of relationships is important in knowing how to fit you in. Hence the bestowal of a title or a kinship term which appears appropriate. It places you within the family and the community. This strong sense of family and community means that individual interests are subordinated to the collective. Hence, there is a higher degree of conformity than in Western societies.

Hot Tip: You May Become an 'Uncle'

The Indonesian sense of family extends to friends and acquaintances. You may find that Indonesians will attempt to draw you into their family circle by bestowing upon you kinship terms such as 'brother' or 'sister' or 'uncle' or 'aunt'. If your acquaintance persists and grows into friendship, you may find yourself drawn also into some of the obligations of family and kinship.

These attitudes to the family and the community affect behaviour in many ways in both private and public life. The business traveller and the casual visitor need to be aware of what constitutes good behaviour if they are to avoid unintentionally giving offence.

IMPORTANCE OF HARMONY

Indonesians place great value upon harmony. If a person behaves according to custom then harmony will prevail and disharmony be avoided. Indonesians dislike a 'scene'. The concept of 'face' is important and no-one should be treated with less than respect in public. Bluntness is rude, loudness is vulgar, aggression is bad manners. One must be sensitive to the feelings of the other person. In the West we think in terms of right and wrong. In Indonesia try to think in terms of what is appropriate and inappropriate in any situation. This applies equally to dress.

For the Westerner, accustomed to getting things done quickly, sweeping aside obstacles and making points firmly and directly, the Indonesian less hurried, more casual approach can be extremely frustrating at times. Losing one's temper is not, in the long run, profitable. You lose respect. The

Hot Tip: Secret of Social Success

In essence, behaviour and dress should not be extreme, should not shock, should maintain harmony. Thus, in all your dealings show courtesy, respect and patience and allow matters to resolve themselves in due course.

best recourse is a sense of humour and acceptance of the elasticity of time.

DRESS

In most of Indonesia, dress is largely determined by the Muslim code of dress, which is that both men and women should dress modestly. In general terms this means that most of the torso and arms and legs should be covered. Clothing should not be tight fitting or revealing. In practical terms, shorts may be worn by children, bathers, cyclists and for sport, but are not acceptable street wear. In private you may wear what you like and in tourist areas and beach resorts brief and scanty clothing is accepted. Conversely, when visiting conservative Muslim areas it is only polite to take care not to offend.

Hot Tip: General Wear for Men & Women

A loose cotton shirt worn either inside or outside loose-fitting trousers, comfortable shoes or sandals. For women, a cotton blouse with long or three-quarter length sleeves and a skirt reaching below the knee, light comfortable shoes or sandals. A bra should be worn at all times.

When conducting business or meeting Indonesians in some official capacity, men should wear a light-weight suit or a long-sleeved shirt and tie. Formal appointments usually require a suit and tie. A below knee-length skirt and smart blouse or a long-sleeved dress are suitable for women, but not trousers.

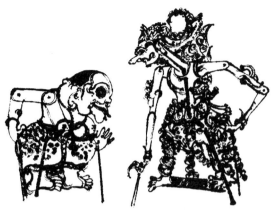

Wayang (shadow play) puppets

For social events like weddings or receptions, dress is usually indicated on the invitation. Men may be permitted to wear a *batik* shirt. These are elaborately patterned cotton shirts and should be worn with long sleeves.

If visiting a mosque, women should cover their heads and legs. Men should not wear shorts. You may be required to don a voluminous gown if improperly dressed, or not allowed in at all. Shoes should be removed. In Bali you will need a scarf to tie around your waist in order to enter a temple. These are often provided at the popular temples.

GESTURES AND BODY LANGUAGE

It is easy to cause offence by making the wrong gesture or adopting a certain stance. There are regional variations, and Indonesians are polite enough to make allowances for foreigners.

However, the following points should enable you to avoid embarrassment:-

- Never give or receive anything with your left hand. The left hand is considered unclean. In a more formal situation, support the right arm at the elbow with the left hand and bow slightly.
- To wave or beckon is considered vulgar. To summon someone, use your right hand with the palm downwards, and make a motion towards yourself with the wrist.
- Do not point with you first finger. Use your thumb to point or your right hand, palm upwards. In some places outside Java, the finger is acceptable, but avoid pointing directly at someone. Never point at anybody with your foot.
- Avoid touching an adult or children on the head. The head is regarded as sacred and should not be referred to directly. If it is necessary to touch a person's head, ask permission first. (Paradoxically, Indonesians are often unable to resist touching the head of a fair haired child!)
- Stand relaxed with your hands clasped either in front or behind. Do not put your hands in your

Tipping

Tipping has become more prevalent, particularly in the cities and tourist areas. In up-market restaurants and hotels, 21 per cent is added to the bill to cover service and tax. Elsewhere you may leave five to ten per cent. Taxi drivers expect the fare to be rounded up, hotel porters expect a small tip for carrying bags and hire-car drivers expect a tip at the end of the trip. If you employ a guide then a tip is also appropriate.

Hot Tip: Observe the Behaviour of your Hosts

Observe carefully the behaviour of your Indonesian hosts and companions. If in doubt, be courteous, self-effacing and restrained. Once Indonesians accept you as a friend, then, in their company, formality may be relaxed.

pockets. Do not lean. Never stand with your hands on your hips as this is a sign of aggression.

- Sit straight when sitting. If you cross your legs do not point your foot at anyone. If required to sit on the floor, men should sit with their legs crossed, women with their legs drawn up to one side. Do not sit with your hands behind your head.

- When introduced to an Indonesian, shake hands with a light grip, giving your name. Many Indonesians, especially Muslims, may raise the right hand towards the heart. A greeting may be emphasized by clasping the offered hand with two hands and bringing both towards the chest.

- When men and women meet, the woman may extend her hand to be taken lightly and momentarily. If a woman does not extend her hand, the man should give a slight nod.

- Remove your shoes when entering a private house.

- When passing in front of a group of seated persons, you should stoop a little, extend your right arm towards the ground and make your way past as unobtrusively as possible.

- If you need to blow your nose, move away to do so. Most Indonesians find the idea of blowing your nose into a handkerchief, which you then put in your pocket or purse, revolting.

- Indonesians have a different sense of private space and you should not be put off or offended by persons sitting close to you or touching you. Except among the more daring youth, persons of the opposite sex usually avoid touching, but persons of the same sex touch a great deal.

- Public displays of affection between persons of the opposite sex are not acceptable.

Crime

Violent crime against visitors is rare, but take care of personal possessions. If your hotel has safety deposit boxes, use them. If you must carry documents, travellers cheques and cards, use a money belt under your clothes, rather than a shoulder bag. Keep a photocopy of your passport, plane tickets and insurance separate from the originals. Report any theft to the police for insurance purposes. BUT: do not be paranoid: use common sense.

3

Religion, Festivals & Public Holidays

Women worship at a mosque in Yogyakarta

Religion permeates Indonesian culture and visitors should treat it with respect. Although Islam is the predominant faith, Hinduism is the major faith on Bali and Christianity is prevalent. Do not be afraid to ask people their religion, for it is a useful guide to how to behave in their presence. It would be improper to offer alcohol to a Muslim and offensive to offer pork.

If visiting a mosque remember that Muslims are expected to pray five times a day – at sunrise, just after the sun has reached its zenith, just before sunset, soon after sunset and again at night. A non-Muslim visitor should avoid visiting a mosque at these times. If invited to or staying in a Muslim household, be careful not to intrude on any person performing prayers.

The art, music and culture of Indonesia are profoundly influenced by the great Hindu epics; the *Ramayana* and the *Mahabharata*. Christians and Moslems know these stories and attend and may dance and act in performances of them. Do not be surprised if someone you have learned is a Muslim or a Christian offers gifts to the spirits before embarking on some enterprise.

Hot Tip: Westerners Are Assumed to be Christian

Indonesians may have few illusions about Westerners, but they will assume that you are Christian or of some other faith. To declare yourself irreligious or an atheist would be greeted with incomprehension and even distress.

All living things are believed to be endowed with a life force known as *semangat*. Indeed this force may also be embodied in sacred objects, a weapon such as the kris, or in places of ritual or sacred significance. In the human it is concentrated in the head and its hair. Many marriage rites in Indonesia include the exchange of locks of hair or the plaiting together of the hair of the bride and groom. The first cutting of an infant's hair is often solemnized by a *selamatan*. Hair (and nail clippings) are important ingredients in spells and potions designed to increase ardour or to work harm and are carefully disposed of lest they fall into the hands of someone who may so use them.

Blood is also imbued with *semangat* and plays a role in many rituals. The ritual battles performed on Flores and Sumba, animal sacrifice, the annointment with blood in some regions of the pillars of newly constructed houses are all indicative of beliefs which in the past involved in some places human as well as animal sacrifice. The tradition that a *kris* (dagger) once drawn must taste blood, and the practice in old Makassar that the royal regalia should be washed in blood, all relate to the belief in blood as a bearer of *semangat*.

More benign are the spirits of plants, most importantly that of the rice plant. Variations of a legend associate the rice spirit with a beautiful woman who preferred death to dishonour and from whose remains the rice plant (and in some versions other food plants) sprang. On Bali she is worshipped as Dewi Sri and temples are dedicated to her. As a consequence, the rice cycle throughout Indonesia is also a religious cycle and ritual directs the whole pattern of the year's farming activity. This respect for the spirits of nature extends to other crops and to hunting and gathering. The purpose is to increase fertility, to ensure good yields, to appease the spirits which inhabit all living things.

Inanimate objects may also acquire *semangat*. Natural features like mountains and lakes; places which are in some way distinctive in form and appearance or are associated with holy or great men or with mythical beings; objects which are in some way distinctive, malformed or out of the ordinary; old artifacts, heirlooms, weapons or treasures: all may contain a soul or spiritual essence which may have to be appeased or revered.

Spirits may be 'good' or 'bad'. Indonesian folk-lore is haunted by *hantu-hantu* or ghosts. These are usually the spirits of those who have suffered a violent death. The billboards garishly advertising Indonesian films reflect a popular genre, equivalent to the Western horror film. A frequent image is that of the *pontianak*, the spirit of a woman who has died in childbirth. Evil spirits like these must be placated or exorcised, which gives occupation to shamans, who also treat ailments and afflictions of various kinds amongst people, livestock and crops. The biggest exorcism of all is held on Bali the day before the Balinese New Year, when evil spirits are driven away with great noise.

FESTIVALS AND PUBLIC HOLIDAYS

These are events and occasions which business travellers may wish to avoid and tourists wish to experience. National holidays are fixed on the Western calendar, but religious holidays are based on the Christian or Muslim calendar, Chinese festivals on the Chinese calendar and festivals in Bali on the Balinese calendar. These are starred on our list. The Muslim holy days (marked [‡]) move back 11 days each year according to the Western calendar.

National Holidays

January 1	**Tahun Baru** – New Year's Day.
December	**Idul Fitri**‡, the end of the fasting month of **Ramadan**.
March/April*	**Good Friday** and **Easter Sunday**
May*	**Idul Adha** – Muslim day of sacrifice commemorating Abraham's willingness to sacrifice his son Isaac.
March*	**Waisak Day** – birth, death and enlightenment of Buddha
May/June*	**Ascension Day**
June/July*	**Muharam**‡ – Muslim New Year
May/June*	**Maulud Nabi Muhammad**‡ – birthday of Muhammad
August 17	**Independence Day**
December*	**Ascension Day of Muhammad**
December 25	**Christmas Day**

OTHER CELEBRATIONS

April 21 Kartini Day – women's day

October Armed Forces Day – celebrates their founding

Ramadan* The ninth month of the Muslim year is a month of fasting, when Muslims fast from dawn to dusk. Many restaurants are closed during the day and you should not eat, drink or smoke in public at this time; and certainly not offer food and drink to Muslims.

January/February* Imlek or Chinese New Year. Most Chinese businesses close for a couple of days.

BALINESE FESTIVALS

There is always a celebration somewhere on Bali. Each of the island's 20,000 temples celebrates an anniversary based on a calendar of 210 days. Also occurring every 210 days is the ten-day Galungan celebration of the triumph of good over evil, the last day of which, Kuningan, being the most important.

March/April* Nyepi, The Balinese New Year. On New Year's Eve evil spirits are driven out with exploding fireworks and the beating of drums. On the day itself, everyone stays quietly indoors to convince the evil spirits that the island is uninhabited and visitors are expected to do the same.

If you are in a tourist area, performances of dance and drama provide some insight into traditional

Borobudur Temple

Balinese culture. However, these lack the spontaneity and involvement of the real thing. Balinese ceremonies from weddings to funerals are communal celebrations. No one will object to your discreet presence, but do not intrude unless invited to participate.

Other islands have festivals which you may ask about when in Indonesia at the time you intend to travel.

RITES OF PASSAGE

All societies celebrate in some form the rites of passage associated with birth, puberty, marriage and death. In Western societies these events have become increasingly private and downgraded, often involving only immediate family. In Indonesia these are communal events in which the whole community (if in a village), or the extended family, friends, neighbours, and business and work associates (if in a town or city) will be involved. These are matters of importance and their proper observance brings honour upon those involved.

They are also matters of spiritual significance. Underlying all belief systems in Indonesia is respect for the spirits which reside in holy places, in objects of nature and in living things. Thus many actions a Westerner considers routine and secular, in Indonesia have a spiritual significance. A Muslim slaughtering an animal will utter a prayer; a farmer harvesting rice will pray or make offerings to the rice spirit; a taxi driver proceeding on a journey may make an offering at a shrine; a businessman before making a decision may seek guidance from a medium. How much more important, therefore, are those events which mark out the life of the individual and of the community. The observance of such events is defined by *adat*, the customary or traditional way of doing things.

A celebration is always accompanied by a feast which brings members of a community together, a tradition still observed in most western societies. The Indonesian word for such a celebration is *selamatan* (safeguarding, with overtones of prosperity and happiness). A *selamatan* is held to mark a birth, circumcision, marriage, a death, an anniversary, the commencement of a new project; or to seek prosperity and good fortune. The basic form on Java is the eating of an inverted cone of coloured rice and ritually slaughtered meats, the recitation of Islamic prayers and the burning of incense. The host makes formal requests and announcements in keeping with the occasion.

MUSLIM CEREMONIES

You may be invited to a *selamatan*, particularly to a wedding feast or *bersanding*, equivalent to the western reception, held after vows have been exchanged. If the family is 'modern' it may be held at a restaurant or hotel; but usually it is at the bride's home to which the bridegroom is escorted in procession. As a guest you can send a small gift of money in a wedding card to the bride's home or pass it discreetly to a member of the bride's family as they stand in line to greet the guests.

The bride and groom will normally be enthroned in rich costumes, to receive the blessings of the guests. As an honoured guest you may be expected to perform the ritual of blessing. You will be shown what to do and will have the opportunity to first observe others. At the end of the ceremony the bride and groom may circulate among the guests who have been seated at tables for the wedding feast. At a traditional wedding men and women will be seated separately and you will be conducted to your seat. At more modern weddings seating may be mixed and the food served buffet-style.

A *selamatan* may be held on other occasions and takes basically the same form. If celebrating a birth, a gift for the baby is in order; if a circumcision, a gift of money to the boy.

Muslims normally bury their dead within twelve hours. The body is prepared by members of the family, the head placed facing Mecca, and passages from the Koran are read over the body. The local Imam will ritually cleanse the body with pure water before it is wrapped in three layers of seamless cloth. Before the face is covered, family and friends view the body for a final farewell and say a silent prayer. Grief is kept under control in public and proceedings are dignified. At the graveyard a pit is dug with a ledge cut into its side. The body is placed in this with its face towards Mecca.

White is the traditional colour of mourning, but sombre dress is acceptable. A white armband may be worn. Refreshments may be served before the ritual cleansing of the body. Flowers may be sent to the home, or a small gift of money in a white envelope may be given.

Hot Tip: Variations Between Regions

Variations in practice occur between regions, between countryside and town and between generations. Seek advice from your Indonesian friends as to what to do and what gifts or sums of money are appropriate. They will appreciate your concern to do the right thing.

PUBLIC *SELAMATAN*

The royal courts at Yogyakarta and Surakarta hold *selamatan* on special occasions. The largest and most popular, known as Sekaten, and coinciding with the prophet Muhammed's birthday, is a spectacular example of how Islam and Javanese tradition have reached accommodation. Thousands of visitors pour into these cities to celebrate a month-long carnival. The culmination is an elaborate and colourful procession through the streets in which courtiers, palace officials and guards, musicians and dancers escort two mountains of rice and vegetables (*gunungan*), representing the ancient fertility symbols, the *lingga* (male) and the *yoni* (female), to the mosque, where they are blessed and the food distributed to the people. Eating it and placing a portion in the fields is said to ensure good health and abundant harvests.

BALINESE CEREMONIES

These have partly been touched on. It is practically impossible to avoid witnessing some aspect of Balinese ritual life during even a short stay in Bali. Apart from the performances put on for tourists, you may come across a procession, a celebration or votaries offering gifts at a shrine.

Balinese Hinduism is distinctly Balinese with pre-Hindu spirits and beliefs incorporated into it. It is also capable of absorbing new deities and forms from outside so that it remains a living belief; in the same way that Balinese art, drama and dance subtly adapt without losing their distinctive style or becoming museum pieces.

Monkey Dance 'Kejak'

Balinese life is guided by ritual. The religious calendar and religious observances structure the day, the year and life itself. The traditional Balinese house is in itself a religious structure in which the family shrine to the ancestors plays an important role. The 'house' consists of a walled enclosure entered by a gateway consisting of two high pillars supporting a roof of thatch. In front, on either side of the gate, are two small shrines for offerings and inside a short wall screens the interior and prevents evil spirits from entering.

Family members live in pavilions around the common courtyard and share a common kitchen and the family temple, which houses the shrine to the ancestors and shrines to other deities. The arrangements of rooms and pavilions is dictated by concepts of hierarchy and auspicious location.

Balinese life is communal. Ritual is subsumed into daily living, within the home and in the village community. A village (*desa*) is itself divided into smaller cooperative neighbourhood groups known as *banjar*, whose members are obliged to support each other during festivals, marriages and funerals. Each *banjar* has a *bale* or communal hall, a drum tower by which to call meetings, a communal kitchen for preparing the feasts which accompany celebrations and performances, a *gamelan* orchestra and dance costumes and a communal temple.

FUNERALS

The Balinese burn their dead in elaborate and expensive ceremonies which may take place within a few days or as long as two years after a person's death. The delay enables the family to gather the money and resources necessary for a satisfactory funeral. In the meantime, the deceased is kept in the house if the time between death and funeral is short; or is buried or mummified if the delay is expected to be long.

After death, rituals are performed to purify the body and to prepare the soul for its final separation from the body over a period of forty-two days. Auspicious days are selected for these and for the cremation of the remains. The cremations are what visitors may see. People of high rank are placed in coffins shaped like bulls if men, cows if women. Other shapes are used for other ranks.

After prayers at the family temple, relatives, guests and villagers gather at the house. War dances are performed to ward of evil spirits, the orchestras, including the *gambang*, only heard at funerals, play through the night. The night passes with a shadow play and readings from the *Bhima Swarga*, the Balinese classic recounting the adventures of Bhima in Hades.

On the day of the funeral, after preparations are complete and a final feast is eaten, the body is taken from the house through or over the compound wall, not through the gate, and carried, twisting and turning in great commotion to confuse the corpse so that it cannot return, to the brightly ornamented wooden and bamboo cremation tower waiting for it.

The uproarious procession of towers proceeds to the cemetery where the bodies are placed into their coffins while relatives crowd around. The high priest conducts the final rites before the fires are lit. The cremation is watched and men stoke the fires and poke the bodies to help them burn. The noise from the crowd and the orchestras is neither solemn nor reverent. The body is no longer important since the soul has left it. As the sun sets and the light fades, the ashes are spread over the waters, the people bathe to cleanse themselves and return to their homes.

Communal ritual, ceremony and celebration has a number of functions. The offerings, sacrifices and prayers assist the passage of the soul to the spirit world and ensure that it will not return to haunt the living. They display respect for and recognition of the dead as a member of the community while living. They also bind the community together and ensure the bereaved of its support.

Hot Tip: You Might Become the Guest of Honour!

Indonesians are friendly and welcoming. If invited to attend a ceremony or festive occasion, even if you a casual passer-by, you may be treated as a guest of honour. Accept with dignity and enjoy the experience. Base your behaviour on what you observe, bearing in mind the religious and cultural susceptibilities of your hosts.

CAMERAS

The camera-laden tourist has become a comic stereotype, but all of us can become unthinking voyeurs through the viewfinder. Indonesia offers a wealth of photogenic opportunities, but remember that the ceremonies and rites which you may stumble across are not staged for your benefit. Unless you are an invited guest, keep a discreet distance. There is always a balance to be struck. In tourist areas there are staged performances and enactments which you may photograph and film at will.

Always ask permission before taking a photograph of a person, unless your telephoto lens is good enough to do so without intrusion. Most Indonesians cannot afford cameras and in some areas will happily be photographed. Unfortunately, they may take this as a very serious and solemn occasion. Usually, however, a quick second shot will catch them relaxed and smiling. If people have allowed you to photograph them take their names and addresses so that copies may be sent – and do so if at all possible. Among Indonesian friends, the situation obviously changes, but remember that you remain a guest. With courtesy, care and discretion you will come away with photographs and film of which you can be proud.

4

Food & Table Manners

Nasi Goreng & Sambal

Many Indonesians are familiar with Western tableware and use it. Younger Indonesians and those who have been abroad will enjoy Western-style food, particularly fast food. Tourist and business hotels provide Western-style menus.

The following remarks apply if you are invited to an Indonesian home or as a guest to an Indonesian restaurant

Indonesians usually use a spoon and a fork. In Indonesian cuisine meat and vegetables are cut small before cooking and are served with rice and in a spicy sauce in plates or bowls placed on the table or, in humbler dwellings, on a mat on the floor. It is good manners to take small portions into your own bowl or plate and to take extra helpings during the course of the meal rather than load your plate at the outset. (This does not necessarily apply at restaurant or hotel buffets, where Indonesians will often load their plates to the brim!)

Hot Tip: Eating By Hand

If required to eat with your hand, remember that only the right hand may be used and the food is taken with your finger tips. It is an acquired skill, but your host will appreciate your efforts; and a spoon will appear if necessary.

Before you start the meal your host will probably direct you to a basin to wash your hands, or provide you with scented water and a towel. Finger bowls will often be placed at the table. If you have been eating with your hands then wash them again at the end of the meal.

To indicate when you have eaten enough, move any uneaten food to one side of your plate (it is good manners to leave something on your plate to show that you have been fully fed) and place your spoon and fork on the plate face downwards and parallel. Toothpicks will usually be on the table. If you need to use one, cover your mouth with your free hand while doing so.

During the meal you will probably be offered water, often warm to indicate that it has been boiled, or tea. You will not usually be offered alcohol. Again, tourist hotels and restaurants are an exception.

Indonesians do not linger over their meals. A meal is usually eaten silently, with little conversation, after which it is usual to retire to the lounge area.

The business traveller may well have cocktail-style functions to attend with canapes and Indonesian-style 'small eats'. These may or may not be served with alcohol and it would be wise to observe what others are drinking before calling for something stronger than fruit juice or a soft drink. Small items like nuts may be taken into the left hand, preferably on a napkin or serviette, and then eaten with the right.

EATING OUT

Hotel restaurants and bars are expensive and there are a great number of eating and drinking places that visitors may try. In the tourist areas there will be some member of staff who can speak English and menus may be in English. A Muslim restaurant may not serve alcohol, but local beer is available in most and is worth trying.

Imported beers and spirits will be available in many restaurants and bars, but wine is less common. In any case, beer and long drinks suit the climate and there is usually a variety of fruit-based drinks and soft drinks for those who do not want alcohol.

STREET VENDORS Wandering vendors may carry a cooking pot and food suspended from a rod carried on their shoulders. More common is a man with a barrow that has a stove and food carried in a glass cabinet on top. Others have a fixed site with a stall, often with a table and stools nearby. Street vendors usually sell such things as rice dishes, noodles, soup, *sate*, icecream and *rujak*, a mixed fruit salad with chilli and peanuts.

SMALL EATING HOUSES These may be called *rumah makan*, *warung* or even *restoran*. The simplest serve a limited range of food. They may display a menu on a board. If not, ask what there is or see what other customers are eating.

RESTORAN PADANG offer a style of eating originally from Padang in Sumatra. They are very common everywhere. There is no menu. You are offered a plate of plain rice and small dishes of spicy meat,

Portable canteen

> ## Hot Tip: Indonesian Food is Hot!
>
> Indonesian food is spicy, with coconut, ginger, peanuts and hot chillies the favourite ingredients. Food is generally served with small saucers of hot chilli sauce (*sambal*) and soy sauce (*kecap*).

fish and vegetables are brought to your table. You pay only for what you eat.

CHINESE RESTAURANTS are found throughout the country. They tend to be slightly more expensive.

WHAT IS THERE TO EAT?

The staple food is rice, although in dryer eastern areas you will find corn, cassava and sweet potato. Seafood and fish (*ikan*) are abundant, freshwater fish is available inland. The most common meats are chicken (*ayam*) and goat (*kambing*). Pork (*babi*) is available in Chinese restaurants and in Hindu, Animist and Christian areas. Vegetables and fruit are plentiful and vegetarians will find soybean cake (*tahu*) and fermented soybeans (*tempe*) are commonly used in Indonesian cooking.

INDONESIAN FAVOURITES

Prawn crackers/fish crackers (*kerupuk udang/ ikan*). A tasty starter by itself or to eat with any spicy dish.

Spicy thick soup (*soto*). Treat as a starter, but often filling enough by itself.

Chicken/goat/beef satay (*sate ayam/kambing/*

daging). Pieces of chicken/goat/beef grilled on skewers over charcoal and served with a spicy peanut dip. On Bali pork satay (*sate babi*) is also available.

Fried rice (*nasi goreng*), rice fried with egg, vegetables and (sometimes) meat

Fried noodles (*mi goreng*)

gado-gado. Mixed vegetables and peanut sauce.

Curry (*kari*). You can get chicken, goat and beef curry without it, but the distinctive and delicious Indonesian curry is made with coconut milk and is known as *gulai*. Try chicken, beef, fish or goat curry – *gulai ayam/daging/ikan/kambing*

Two dryer spicy dishes are spiced chicken cooked slowly in coconut milk (*rendang ayam*) and beef cooked very slowly in coconut milk and spices (*rendang daging sapi*).

At tourist resorts you may be offered the *rijstaffel*, (rice table), a relic of Dutch colonial cuisine, which is a buffet of many dishes. This is a good way to find out what many dishes are. Do not be afraid to ask their Indonesian names for future reference.

The range of food and flavours is wide and variable across the country. Those mentioned are the most common, but be prepared to ask for the local speciality.

What is the local speciality? Say: *Akan makanan spesial daerah ini?*

5

Doing Business

Function room, Jakarta hotel

In business terms, traditional family and communal attitudes operate in two ways. Indonesians believe in the importance of social harmony. Social harmony is dependent upon the inner spiritual harmony of individuals and regard for the feelings of others.

Indonesians believe in consensus. In private life this means reaching unanimous agreement after consultation with family, friends and colleagues. In public life and business there is a similar striving for consensus, which, in the Western view, may take numerous meetings and an inordinate amount of time.

Hot Tip: Learn the Key Words!

Indonesians enjoy meetings. Learn and understand these words and the principles they embody:

Gotong royong	mutual cooperation, working together
muafakat	consensus, mutual agreement
mesyuarat	discussion, mutual exchange of views with respect for individual feelings and avoidance of loss of face (see below).

PATRON/CLIENT RELATIONS

In the family, relations between individuals are defined by their relative position in the family structure. In business and professional life, and in politics, relations are defined by personal relationships within the hierarchy which may be based on family or regional ties, or upon personal obligations for services rendered. In business, loyalties are personal to the *bapak*, or boss rather than to the organization itself. The term (bapak; father) is indicative of this personal factor.

It is easy to see how a system of patron/client relationships is developed, whereby those with position, wealth and prestige provide for the less fortunate and receive their loyalty in return, thus increasing their prestige. It is a system open to nepotism, corruption and cronyism: but it also provides support and security for the client.

THE INDONESIAN CHINESE

Indonesian business enterprise owes a great deal to the input of the Indonesian Chinese. This influence is readily discernible in the commercial and business districts where Chinese shops and premises are evident. It is also involved in larger enterprises where its presence may not be so easily recognized. Many of Chinese origin have accepted Islam and have abandoned their Chinese names. They have usually entered into joint operations with non-Chinese Indonesian partners.

The Chinese traditional social structure is based upon the patriarchal extended family. Business relationships throughout the region are often channelled through companies in which members of the extended family, settled elsewhere within and without Indonesia, have a controlling voice. The Chinese business structure is patterned on the family structure, and based on kinship, loyalty and subservience. Under a façade of modernization these loyalties affect decision-making.

The combination of traditional Indonesian family and patron/client relationships on the one hand and Chinese kinship loyalties on the other, require the outsider to exercise caution.

Hot Tip: Find the Seat of Power!

Ascertain who holds the real authority and power. Not all may be as it seems and the decision-makers may not be immediately obvious. Treat contacts with courtesy and patience, for you, too, will be being observed and assessed.

BUSINESS HOSPITALITY

Indonesians like to know with whom they are dealing. They will wish to know about you personally; your character, your family, your background, your status. Social occasions are opportunities for them to get to know you and if matters are proceeding well you may be invited to their homes. This hospitality places you under obligations which require you to reciprocate. On the other hand, social occasions enable you to get to know your potential Indonesian partners.

Indonesians prefer personal face-to-face business negotiations. The phone, fax and e-mail can carry you so far, but personal contact builds confidence and trust which, once established, are more important than a signature on a contract.

This contact is usually arranged through inter-mediaries who understand the correct channels of communication and can carry out informal negotiations before official neetings and nego-tiations occur. If your business is new to Indonesia, then establishing the right contact is a high priority.

Hot Tip: Observe the Social Pleasantries

At what you may consider purely a business meeting, remember the social pleasantries. Do not proceed immediately to business, nor show impatience at delay. Conversation and social exchange are means of getting to know and trust the other prior to settling business matters for the longer term.

GIVING AND RECEIVING GIFTS

The giving and receiving of gifts is a delicate matter. Each situation has to be judged on its merits, but, generally, hospitality and gifts should be roughly matched. Remember that gifts of alcohol are inappropriate for a Muslim. Sweets, flowers, ornamental objects, particularly items from your own country, are appreciated. Be wary of giving or receiving expensive items like jewelry.

Your Indonesian business associates will often have family or social links to local and national political elites. The separation of interests is not always clear. Former politicians, civil servants and military personnel are often connected with private and state business enterprises. It is best to be aware of these connections, but to confine your business dealings with your actual or prospective business partners.

For this reason, and because of the emphasis placed on personal dealings in business relations, it is important to check out the credentials of potential business partners and their companies. Be wary of those who provide lavish hospitality and gifts and then offer contacts and information at a price.

THE BUREAUCRACY

Indonesian bureaucracy exists to see that procedures are followed. Government officials see themselves as in positions of authority and expect to be treated with respect. They may be civil, but they are not your servants. Be respectful, defer to their advice and the procedures laid down, and you will be courteously treated. To show irritation and impatience serves no purpose.

Businesses employ gophers or intermediaries to deal with government officials. As an individual you may at some time be required to have personal dealings with customs or immigration or other officials. In such cases the advice is to get to the office concerned early with all your paperwork and a book to read, wait your turn and be philosophical if some error or change in procedure renders the visit fruitless. Time is not an issue. There is always another day.

6

Getting Around, Shopping & Health Matters

Bajaj (three-wheeled taxi)

The Indonesian climate is generally hot and humid and westerners unaccustomed to it generally find walking any long distance sweaty and tiring. In the highlands the climate is much more equable and walking can be pleasant. Most visitors, however, will need to use some form of transport.

BY ROAD

Tourists and business travellers may find their transport needs largely catered for by their tour operators or business hosts. You can also try private hire, ranging from a car with driver to a self-driven car to a motor-bike. Traffic drives on the left, the maximum speed limit is 60 kph (45 mph), and you need to carry at all times your international driver's license and the registration documents of the vehicle. Motor cyclists must wear helmets.

This is all straightforward, but driving in most places is not. The roads are crowded and whatever the law may say, the size and weight of vehicle determines right of way. While there are good trunk roads, including toll roads, driving on them is often very fast and erratic. Other roads may be in a very poor condition.

If you are at all of a nervous disposition, it is advisable to employ a driver. Negotiate payment for the trip and the time you wish to take. You will be expected to pay for the meals and accommodation of the driver, but these costs are reasonable.

Taxis operate in the cities and towns. In Jakarta and larger centres they are metered, but check that the meter is on. Elsewhere, be prepared to bargain. If staying for a few days and satisfied with your driver, then bargain for his services for the duration of your stay.

Inter-city taxis/mini-buses are a convenient way of travelling between nearby cities, for instance from Jakarta to Bandung, Bogor or Cirebon.

For short distances try the 'bajaj', a three-wheel motorized vehicle which will whisk you noisily through the traffic, or a bicycle rickshaw (trishaw) known as the 'becak'. In heavy traffic this can be

Hot Tip: Never Leave Home Without It!

Always carry with you the written address of your destination, and directions if you can obtain them, the address of where you are staying and the telephone numbers.

nerve-wracking, but at quieter times and in the evening it is a leisurely and pleasant means of getting around. If in a place for an extended period it is advisable to employ the same *becak* and to settle on an agreed price. On first use of a *becak* be prepared to bargain.

Local bus services are usually crowded and uncomfortable, but they are cheap and certainly a way to meet the locals, and often their livestock. Luggage is tied to the roof under a tarpaulin, so take into the bus anything you may need on the journey. If possible, board at the bus station, where you have the opportunity to choose a seat. Indonesians are generally slighter than Europeans so three will squeeze into the space for two, and a European may well lack leg room.

Buses tend to fill up from the rear, so do not be alarmed if a person sits beside you when there are empty seats still available. **Warning:** Jakarta has more than one bus station. Check which one you are to use.

Minibuses, often converted vans or trucks, are found everywhere under various names – 'bemos', 'colts', 'microlets', 'oplets'. These are also cheap, but crowded.

Long-distance express buses, often air-conditioned and comfortable, operate between cities, and, via ferry services, between islands. Night express buses or '*bis malam*' are convenient options. In some places, such as between Solo and Yogyakarta, express buses run at regular intervals and drop you at your hotel or *losman* (guesthouse) if asked.

Privately-owned tourist buses operate in and between tourist areas. They are comfortable and convenient, but more expensive.

BY RAIL

Services are restricted to Java and parts of Sumatra. Visitors will most probably use the Java service. There are three classes of travel: First-class, with air-conditioning (not always available); second class, with fans, and third class. Some overnight express trains have sleepers and reclining seats.

Express Trains

The two main express trains are the *Bima Express* and the *Mutiara Utara Express*, both running daily each way between Jakarta (Kota Station) and Surabaya.

Bima Express: Jakarta – Yogyakarta – Solo – Surabaya (Gubeng Station)

Mutiara Utara: Jakarta – Cirebon – Tegal – Pekalongan – Semarang – Surabaya (Pasar Turi Station)

From Surabaya one may take a ferry to Bali.

Tickets must be bought at the point of and on the day of departure, although some night express tickets may be bought a day in advance. Travellers may prefer to pay extra to obtain tickets through a tourist office rather than deal with the chaos often encountered at railway stations. **Warning:** Check which rail station your service leaves from.

BY AIR

In remote areas not served by a domestic airline travellers may book seats (subject to availability) or arrange charters with The Mission Aviation Fellowship or Associated Mission Aviation which serve Christian mission staff.

Internal air fares are reasonable, with concessions for children up to twelve years.

Garuda offer a Visit Indonesia Air Pass to those entering the country on Garuda. The pass must be booked outside the country or within 14 days of arrival. The pass enables you to buy three one way flights and to obtain other flights at a reduced rate.

Hot Tip: Never Take your Flight for Granted!

Always confirm your booked flights 24–72 hours in advance at each stop. Also, flights are often over-booked, cancelled or delayed. In practice, except for return tickets, you need to be in a place before you can book a ticket out of it. Be prepared for delays and allow for them in your planning.

BY SEA

The national line PELNI operates services throughout the archipelago. The larger ships offer first class (en suite cabins with TV), second class and economy passages. Prices are reasonable.

Vehicle ferries operate between the main islands.

Smaller islands are served by small craft of various kinds, often overloaded and dubiously seaworthy. However, thousands of journeys are made without mishap, there is often no other option, and the voyage will be memorable.

BY RIVER

River transport is still the only option in many places, particularly in Kalimantan. River craft vary in size, speed and comfort with regular services operating on some stretches. For a long trip up-river take a sleeping mat, food and bottled water. The

Hot Tip: Understand the Indonesian 'clock'!

Indonesians operate to a different sense of time. Punctuality is not a matter of great concern. Be prepared to go with the flow.

Carry with you the book you have long wanted to read but for which you have not had the time. You will almost certainly finish it.

If you retain your sense of humour and remain relaxed, travel in Indonesia is an experience you will long remember.

boats have kitchens or may stop for meals, but the variety of food lessens the further one goes into the interior. There may be accommodation on land at night.

ACCOMMODATION

Accommodation ranges from five-star international hotels to the humbler inn ('*wisma*') or guesthouse ('*losmen*'). Business travellers or tourists will have accommodation booked for them. If you are arriving independently, it is advisable to pre-book accommodation at a recognized hotel for your first couple of nights, after which you may look elsewhere. Moderately priced accommodation is usually, clean, comfortable, friendly and, perhaps more to the point, Indonesian.

INDONESIAN PLUMBING

If you stay in hotels and tourist accommodation or use facilities in modern office blocks and the houses of the well-to-do, you will find the bathroom and toilet fixtures you are used to, although there is more likely to be a shower cubicle than a bath. In older houses and cheaper accommodation and places off the beaten track you will meet the squat toilet. This consists of a hole in the floor with foot places on either side. Most that you may have occasion to use will be of enamel and flushed from a tank in the way that you are used to.

The cubicle may be small for a European and the floor may be wet. This is because toilet paper is not used (it would block the plumbing) and cleansing is done with water, from a tap or receptacle placed conveniently to hand. Modern versions can take paper, or there may be a lidded container to receive used paper.

Usually, there will be a pair of sandals or thongs placed outside to wear, and a hook behind the door for clothing. Remember, however awkward and put-off you may feel, the squat toilet is hygienic, in that no part of the anatomy touches unclean surfaces.

Should you use a traditional Indonesian bathroom or 'tempat mandi' you may find it has been fitted with a shower. If not, there will be a large tank of water set against one wall and a dipper with which to take water and wash yourself from the top down. The water may be cold, but in the Indonesian climate this is no hardship and the process refreshing.

Batik textile design

The daring traveller who goes into the countryside and remoter areas may have to use a stand-pipe or bathe in a river. At such times, men wear loose shorts or a sarong and women cover themselves with a sarong. Toilet facilities may be less screened than one is used to. You should remember that no-one will pay the least attention. In Indonesia, shame attaches to the person looking, not to the person performing the action.

SHOPPING

Unless staying for a considerable time, you will mainly be shopping for souvenirs or gifts. Hotel shops are expensive and for basic toiletries and other items you may wish to buy outside. Supermarkets and department stores are fixed price and easy to shop in. They also give you an idea of prices for when you may wish to shop in the market.

Visitors often feel suspicious about the prices they are charged. Generally, bargaining over a bar of soap is not worth attempting and necessities will be sold to you at a fair price. Bargaining enters into it when it is a more expensive item like, perhaps, a scarf or length of batik which catches your eye.

Indonesia has a great variety of arts and artifacts. These may easily be obtained from fixed price shops, but you may wish to look further. In particular:

Textiles

BATIK Molten wax is applied to fabric to prevent dye penetrating the cloth, those portions of the fabric free of wax accepting the dye. By repeating the process many times complex patterns of many colours may be produced. The most famous batik centres are Solo and Yogakarta in central Java and Pekalongan in northern Java.

ITAK The threads are tied and dyed before weaving producing attractive designs with slightly blurred outlines. Produced in many parts of Indonesia including Sumatra, Java, Sulawesi, Kalimantan, Bali and Nusa Tenggara.

SONGKET The patterns and motifs are woven into the cloth with gold and silver thread. Sumatra and Bali are important areas.

BARKCLOTH, produced in the highland areas of Kalimantan, Sulawesi and Irian Jaya, is made by pulping the bark of suitable plants and beating it into sheets, which are then decorated.

ARTS AND CRAFTS

Look for pottery and basket-ware, wood carvings, the ceremonial dagger or 'kris' which differs in design of both hilt and blade in different parts of Indonesia, and metal work. Stone carving is a feature of Bali, which also produces the more elaborate form of *kris*. Modern woodcarving is well-developed in Java and Bali. More 'primitive' styles are produced in Kalimantan, Sulawesi and Irian Jaya.

Bali is renowned for its art and artists colonies. Ubud is the centre for art with many galleries with work for sale. Yogyakarta on Java has a similar reputation. In both places look also for the leather puppets which are used in the *wayang* or shadow play.

Jewellery, mainly of silver and semi-precious stones, is produced. Bali is an important centre. Unless you know what you are doing, it is best to buy from reputable stores attached to the hotels.

ANTIQUES

Genuine antiques are expensive and to be sure of what you are getting stick to reputable shops. There are also laws forbidding the export of antiques which may have come from an archae-ological site. Fake antiques – amulets, carvings, ceramics, artifacts, fabrics, beads and other items are produced and 'aged' for the tourist market. They make attractive and interesting souvenirs – and occasionally you may be lucky – but do not place much trust in guarantees of their provenance unless from a reputable source.

TOUTS

Usually, these are young men who receive a commission from a shop, hotel, *losman*, restaurant or taxi/bus company. They often have good English and are knowledgeable. Generally, they are best ignored, as politely as possible.

HEALTH MATTERS

As a visitor you will have no immunities to even relatively mild local diseases and ailments, so precautions are necessary before and during your visit, if it is not to be spoiled by illness. Make sure that you have adequate medical insurance as part of your travel insurance package.

Inoculations

No inoculations are legally required before you enter Indonesia, unless you arrive from a country which has yellow fever. In that case you must have a certificate of immunization.

If you are travelling out of the main tourist areas, inoculations are advisable for typhoid, tetanus, polio and hepatitis A. For certain areas, inoculation against Hepatitis B, rabies and Japanese encephalitis may also be advised. Consult your doctor and travel and travel adviser well in advance as some inoculations require a series of injections over a period of time.

Malaria

Malaria is endemic and requires a programme of drugs beginning at least a week before you go and continuing for up to four weeks after your return. The drug prescribed will depend upon the area to which you are going because certain strains of malaria are resistant to some drugs. Consult your doctor well in advance. Carry mosquito repellant with you or purchase immediately on your arrival.

Intestinal disorders

Most travellers experience some diarrhoea if only because of the change in diet and climate. It will quickly pass and nothing serious will eventuate if proper precautions are taken. Carry a supply of tablets with you to use at the first signs of discomfort. Pharmacies in Indonesia also carry several brands. Take in plenty of fluid to avoid dehydration. Pharmacies also carry rehydration salts.

Drinking water

Tap water is unsafe throughout Indonesia. Drink only bottled water (*air mineral*), which is available almost everywhere, or water which has been boiled for at least five minutes or has been filtered and chemically sterilized. Avoid ice in your drinks. Drinks made with boiling water, such as tea or coffee, are safe, as are beer and brand-named mixes and soft drinks.

Exposure to the sun

Because of the humidity it is easy to underestimate the power of the sun. Take the usual precautions of covering up, wearing a hat, using sun cream, and taking fluid and extra salt to counteract sweating. Avoid the sun during the hottest part of the day.

Medical facilities

The major cities and tourist areas have reasonable medical facilities. Hotels often have a doctor on call or can put you in touch with one. Elsewhere, medical centres and clinics vary and many have limited resources. Most towns have well-stocked pharmacies at which you can buy a wide range of drugs and medicines. It is advisable to carry sufficient quantities of any medicines you use regularly.

Passport and visa requirements

Your passport must be valid for at least six months from the date of entry. Make sure that it is.

Nationals of many countries, including the United Kingdom, Ireland, the United States, Canada, Australia and New Zealand, do not need visas if in possession of a ticket for an onward or return journey and entering the country at one of the approved entry points. Entry by this means is for 60 days, non-renewable. However you may leave the country and then enter again through one of the approved gateways.

Business visas may be obtained on application. These are for five weeks and are renewable at the discretion of the immigration authorities.

Top Tip 1. Entry requirements may change. Always check with your travel agent, an Indonesian Embassy or consular office, or an Indonesian tourist promotion office. The latter will also have publications and maps.

Top Tip 2. Most people enter through Jakarta. It is worth checking in Singapore for one month excursion flights with Singapore Airlines or Garuda.

7

The Regions

Terraces, Bali

For administrative purposes, Indonesia is divided into 27 administrative districts, but tourists and casual travellers may think in terms of eight regions based on the main islands or island groups: **Sumatra**, **Java**, **Bali**, **Kalimantan** (Borneo), **Nusa Tenggara** (the old Lesser Sunda Islands), **Sulawesi** (Celebes), **Maluku** (Moluccas) and **Irian Jaya** (West New Guinea).

Business travellers may need to deal with the provincial authorities, as may other travellers who run into difficulties. The provinces and their administrative capitals within each region are listed in the summaries below.

SUMATRA

Provinces

Aceh, capital Bandar Aceh

Sumatera Utara (North Sumatra), capital Medan

Sumatera Barat (West Sumatra), capital Padang

Riau, capital Pekanbaru

Jambi, capital Jambi

Bengkulu, capital Bengkulu

Sumatera Selatan (South Sumatra), capital Palembang

Lampung, capital Telukbetung.

Main points of interest

Sumatra is the world's sixth largest island and is about 1,000 miles long. Its main attractions are its often spectacular scenery and indigenous cultures.

Most visitors fly into Medan to visit the **Batak Highlands** and **Lake Toba** (Danau Toba), at just over 1,700 square metres (635 square miles) the largest lake in Southeast Asia. It lies some 100 kilometres south of Medan at a height of 900 metres within the crater of a prehistoric volcanic eruption and is up to 450 metres deep. Visit it for the mountain scenery, cool climate and picturesque Batak villages.

Another area of spectacular natural beauty and cultural significance is the Minangkabau region of West Sumatra, stretching inland from

Padang on the coast to the hill station of **Bukittinggi**. The Minankabau are remarkable for being staunch Muslims who have retained their traditional matrilineal society.

Bengkulu was for a time a British trading station and Fort Marlborough, constructed in 1762, still stands. Sir Stamford Raffles, founder of Singapore, was Lieutenant Governor from 1818–1823. The Dendam Taksuda Botanical Gardens contain the giant Rafflesia flower named after him.

Palembang's past as the capital of a great maritime empire is not reflected in great architectural monuments, but the Rumah Bari Museum contains megalithic, Hindu and Buddhist statuary, while the traditional music and dance has forms which date back to the seventh century. These days, Palembang's wealth comes from oil and the petrochemical industry.

JAVA

Provinces

Jakarta, capital of Indonesia and administrative centre for its immediate environs.

Jawa Barat (West Java), capital Bandung

Jawa Tengah (Central Java), capital Semarang

Jawa Timur (East Java), capital Surabaya

Main points of interest

The island, about the size of England, is remarkably fertile, its soils enriched by the volcanic ash ejected from its 121 volcanic cones in the past. Some 30 of these are still active and eruptions continue at intervals bringing death and destruction but also a renewal of fertility. Consequently, the island supports 60 per cent of Indonesia's total population at a density of over 800 people per square kilometre (2000 per square mile). Even so, areas of wilderness and calm may still be found.

Taman Mini or the 'Indonesia In Miniature Park' provides a taste of what the country has to offer. Situated on the southern outskirts of Jakarta it has 27 pavilions dedicated to each of Indonesia's provinces and built, using traditional materials and methods, to reflect the regional style of architecture. Inside each are displays of artifacts, costumes, handicrafts and cultural items of the region. These are built around a lake containing a three-dimensional relief map of the Indonesian archipelago.

North Java is often overlooked by visitors, but has much to offer. **Cirebon's** two palaces, the Kraton Kesepuhan and Kraton Kanoman, date from 1678, the Grand Mosque (Mesjid Ageng), from c.1500. Outside Cirebon is the **Taman Arum Sunyaragi**. Built as a fortress against the Dutch in 1702, it was redesigned in coral, mortar and stone by a Chinese architect in 1852 as a garden retreat for pleasure and meditation for Cirebon's rajas. Cirebon is famous also for its nearby villages of artists and artisans.

The city of **Pekalongan**, 220 kilometres east of Cirebon, is famous for its batiks. **Semarang** has

Downtown Java

an extensive old Chinatown while **Rembang** and **Lassem** are probably the oldest Chinese settlements on Java. From Semarang you can reach the hill resort of **Bandungan** and the temples at **Gedung Songo**, built in the eighth century on a spectacular mountain site and dedicated to Siva.

A day trip takes you to the temples and lakes of the Dieng Plateau, while the adventurous may wish to climb **Mount Merapi**. Surakarta is quieter but there is much to see, including the two palaces, the **Museum Radya Karawiton** and the **Akademi Seni Karawiton Indonesia** where, in the afternoons, you may watch gamelan and dance practices. Shopping in the markets and shops is unhurried. Visit the **Pasar Klewer**, near the Grand Mosque, for textiles and **Pasar Triwindu** for 'antiques' and bric-a-brac. Outside the city, **Candi Sukuh** and **Candi Ceto**, are dramatically sited on the slopes of Gunung Lawu.

Both cities are repositories of Javanese culture and the courts keep alive the court traditions in music, dance and drama. The Javanese drama tradition stems from the popular shadow play (*wayang kulit*) where the shadows of flat leather puppets are thrown against a screen by the puppeteer who provides also the dialogue. Actors perform *wayang orang* or dance drama (literally *orang* means 'man') and *wayang topeng*, mask drama. Hotels provide truncated performances of traditional dance and drama for tourists.

BALI

Bali, capital Denpasar

Bali is a major tourist destination: those looking for surf, sand, night-life and shopping head for **Kuta**; those with more sedate tastes for **Sanur**. Both are on the southern coast. Inland is **Ubud** a centre for artists both Balinese and foreign. It is set in beautiful hill country and spectacular rice terraces, its surrounding villages specializing in different crafts and art forms.

Further north, **Lake Batur**, the largest lake in Bali, lies in the crater of a massive eruption. There are spectacular views into the crater from its rim at

Penelokan and it is possible to descend to the lake by a narrow road and to take a boat to **Trunyan**, one of the few surviving villages of the Bali Aga, pre-Hindu Balinese. Visit the temple of **Pura Ulun Danu** perched on the crater rim. At **Kintamani**, further along the rim, a market is held every three days. It is possible to climb Gunung Batur and to visit its four craters.

The cultural life of Bali is a major tourist attraction and dances and drama performances are regularly performed to the accompaniment of the *gamelan*. Among the most popular are the graceful *Legong* dance, the *Baris* war dance, the *Kecak* or monkey dance, and the *Barong*, a dance drama.

The highest and most sacred mountain on Bali is **Gunung Agung** on the eastern side of the island, the site of Bali's most powerful kingdoms. Travelling from the south all roads pass through **Gianyar**, the weaving centre of Bali, to **Klungkung**, the site of Bali's most important kingdom, noted for its eighteenth century **Kerta Gosa** or Hall of Justice with its ceiling murals and the **Bale Kambang** or floating pavilion.

North of Klungkung, past spectacular rice terraces, is the **Pura Besakih** temple, Bali's holiest shrine, a complex of twenty-two temples on the lower slopes of Gunung Agung.

Also on the east coast, several kilometres inland, is **Tenganan**, the main village of the Bali Aga, with their distinctive culture and traditions, who have provided a cautious welcome to visitors only within the past twenty years. At and near **Amlapura** are the palaces and hydraulic creations of the last king of what was then known as Karangasem, whom the Dutch permitted to retain his title and powers.

NUSU TENGGARA

Provinces

Nusa Tenggara Barat (Lombok and Sumbawa), capital Mataram (on Lombok)

Nusa Tenggara Timur (Sumba, Flores, Timor and adjacent islands), capital Ende (on Flores)

EAST TIMOR

East Timor has acquired independence from Indonesia and travellers wishing to go there should make enquiries in their own country before they attempt to do so.

Lombok has a mainly Muslim population and is drier and less densely inhabited than Bali. Its culture is a mixture of Muslim and Hindu. **Mataram** is the administrative centre, but most of the cultural and architectural attractions are within easy reach of **Cakranegara**, the old royal capital. Visit the **Pura Meru** temple, the **Pura Mayura** royal gardens, and the unassuming royal palace. Nearby temples with impressive views are at **Mount Pengsong** and **Batu Bolong**. At **Narmada** is a nineteenth-century palace and garden complex built by the Balinese King of Karangasem. **Sweta Market** is the place for buying local craft and artifacts.

Lombok has many long, largely deserted beaches on the south coast, but **Senggigi** is the most developed resort. The small offshore islands of **Gill Air**, **Gill Meno** and **Gill Trawangan** provide diving and snorkelling in clear waters. The mountain resorts of **Tetebatu** and **Sapit** are restful, or you may be tempted to scale **Gunung Rinjani**, Indonesia's third highest peak. Less testing is the climb to the beautiful crater lake of **Segara Anak**.

Between Sumbawa and Flores is the island of **Komodo**, where the largest monitor lizard in the world, has become a tourist attraction.

The mountain of **Krell Mutu** in Southern Flores has three crater lakes which change colour for no apparent reason.

Sumba is off the beaten track. Its main attraction is the annual Pasola ceremony during which ritual fights take place between groups of armed horsemen in the days following the full moon in the second or third lunar month. Check dates before you travel.

KALIMANTAN (BORNEO)

Provinces:

Kalimantan Barat, capital Pontianak

Kalimantan Tengah, capital Banjermasin

Kalimantan Timur, capital Balikpapan

Kalimantan is sparsely populated. The coastal areas are swampy so that the few large cities are many kilometres inland on the banks of the major rivers, on the sites of early Muslim Sultanates. These are inhabited mainly by Malays and Chinese. Transmigration schemes have resettled thousands of Javanese and Balinese peasants with varying success. The interior is inhabited by Dayak peoples, whose traditional way of life is under pressure. Kalimantan supplies most of Indonesia's oil and timber and the exploitation of its resources is poorly controlled.

Pontianak offers access to the **Kapuas River**. A road links it to **Singkawan**, which has fine beaches and Chinese temples, and to Sambas known for its fine cloth. The **Mandor National Park** has a botanical garden, war memorial and orchid gardens.

Banjarmasin situated 22 kilometres up the **Barito River** is built on a network of rivers and canals. Most of its houses are on stilts. Of interest are **Sabilia Muhtadin Mosque**, the early morning floating market, the old harbour (**Pelabuhan Lama**) and the **Ceramic Museum**. Banjermasin is the centre of the Indonesian gem trade and **Martapura**, 25 kilometres to the east, the centre specifically for diamonds, can be reached by motorized canoe.

Within reach of **Banjarmasin** are the **Pulau Kaget** (to see proboscis monkeys) and the **Pleihari Martapura** National Parks. **Balikpapan** is an oil town. **Samarinda**, 60 kilometres up the **Mahakam** River, can be reached from Balikpapan by air or by road and river. More interesting than either of these is **Tenggarong**, one-time capital of the Sultan of Kutei. The palace is now the **Mulawarman Museum**, housing ceramics, royal regalia and Dayak artifacts. From Tenggarong trips are organized up the Mahakam into Dayak country.

SULAWESI

Provinces

Sulawesi Utara (North Sulawesi), capital Manado

Sulawesi Tengah (Central Sulawesi), capital Palu

Sulawesi Selatan (South Sulawesi), capital Ujung Pandang

Sulawesi Tenggara (Southeast Sulawesi), capital Kendari

Sulawesi's starfish shape makes overland travel difficult, but there is much of interest. **Ujung Pandang**, once known as Macassar, was the capital of the commercial empire of the Bugis until the Dutch captured it. **Fort Rotterdam**, is now a museum, but Bugis boats still dock at **Paotere**.

Inland from **Parepare** is the land of the Toraja, a mainly Christian people who have retained their distinctive boat-shaped houses and complex and expensive funeral ceremonies, which take place sometimes years after death. These last for up to a week and are performed mainly in July and August, but also in May and June, at which time there are fewer tourists. *Tau-tau*, life-size effigies of the dead, are placed in galleries high above the plain in cliffside galleries. The main centre is **Rantepao**. The area provides good walking and local transport is good.

Central Sulawesi is difficult of access but attractions are the **Bada Valley** with its large stone megaliths, **Lake Poso**, and the **Lore Lindu National Park**.

MALUKU

Maluku Utara (North Maluku) including the spice islands of Ternate and Tidore and the large island of Halmahera

Maluku Tengah (Central Maluku) including Baru, Ceram, Ambon and the Bandars, capital Kota Ambon which is the administrative centre for the whole Maluku region.

Maluku Tenggara (Southeast Muluku)

Manado and North Sulawesi are more easily accessible with direct flights from Singapore. Attractions include the **Bunaken-Manado Marine National Park**, which offers superb diving and snorkelling, the **Tangkoko Batuangus National Park, Lake Tondano**, and the **Taman Anggrek Orchid Garden** at Airmaddi.

Sulawesi is developing its infrastructure and there are numerous places of great scenic beauty and cultural interest which tourist offices will direct you to.

Maluku has great natural beauty and numerous relics of its colonial past. The island of **Ambon** is largely Christian. Kota Ambon was founded by the Portuguese in 1574 and then taken by the Dutch. Some colonial remnants such as **Fort**

Victoria and the residence of the Dutch governor survive. The **Museum Siwalima** houses tribal artifacts and other items. In caves near **Kusukusu Serah** are ancient megaliths, still found outside some villages.

The **Banda Islands** have old Dutch forts, beaches, reefs and Mount Api to explore. **Ternate** and **Tidore** are two volcanic cones rising some 1,700 metres from the sea about a kilometre apart. Portuguese, Spanish, Dutch and, briefly, English, traded and competed with the native sultans and fortifications litter the coast. The **Kedaton** in Ternate, the palace of the last sultan, is now a museum. The islands offer diving, snorkelling, walking, climbing and spectacular scenery.

IRIAN JAYA

Irian Jaya, capital Jayapura

Irian Jaya is Indonesia's largest province, mountainous, sparsely populated, its interior until recently largely untouched by the outside world. The desire to exploit its minerals, oil, timber and fishing resources are rapidly changing that. You need a *surat jalan* to travel outside Jayapura, Biak and Sorong. You will need to present to the police four passport photos, list the places you wish to travel to and report to the local police on your arrival. Much of the country is out of bounds partly because the *Organasi Papua Merdeka* or Papuan Freedom Movement has been fighting a war of independence since the 1960s.

Jayapura (then Hollandia) was General MacArthur's Pacific Headquarters and the wreckage of several war-time ships may be seen on the beaches of **Yotefu National Park**, east of Jayapura. The Anthropological Museum at Cendrawasih University in Abepura, near Jayapura, has a collection of Iranese tribal artifacts, including prized Asmat carvings. **Wamena** in the Baliem Valley in the highlands and home of the Dani people, is accessible by air from Jayapura. **Agats**, on the south coast is open to tourists. The Museum of Culture and Progress displays Asmat carving and up-river trips may be arranged.

8

Speaking the Language

Traditional dance

The national language is Bahasa Indonesia, a standardized Malay almost identical to that adopted by Malaysia, Brunei and Singapore. It has taken words from a variety of sources – Sanskrit, Arabic, Chinese, Portuguese, Dutch and English. Pronunciation presents few problems for European language speakers and it is relatively easy to acquire a working vocabulary. The written form has been romanized and is easy to read.

Hot Tip: It's Worth It!

Although English is the language of business and tourism, and Indonesians will want to practise their English upon you, they are delighted when visitors use their language and it is worth learning the basic greetings and courtesies.

English speakers are rare outside the tourist and business centres. You will find that a number of words are familiar, having been taken from English and given an Indonesian spelling.

The following notes on pronunciation are a guide to standard Bahasa Indonesia. In practice you will find regional variations and considerable elision make understanding what is said difficult. However, once you show a willingness to try speaking the language, Indonesians will happily slow their speech and standardize their pronunciation.

Consonants are as in English, with these exceptions.

b   at the end of a word like 'p' in 'gap'
c   like 'ch' in 'church'
d   at the end of a word like 't' in 'hat'
f   pronounced as in 'fat' but often replaced by 'p'
g   always hard as in 'get'
h   Between two different vowels pronounced lightly or not at all: **tahu** (know) – tau
k   at the end of words like a glottal stop: **tidak** (not/no) – tida'
kh   like 'ch' in 'loch'

ng   as in 'singer'
ngg   as in 'linger'
ny   as in 'bunion'
sy   like 'sh' in 'ship': syarikat (a company) –
      'sharikat'

Vowels in open syllables are pronounced differently
from those in closed syllables.

a   open syllables – like 'u' in 'up': **apa** (where)
           closed syllables – slightly shorter: **makan** (to
           eat) mahkan
e   when unstressed as in 'open'
           when stressed as in 'bed'
i   open syllables – like 'ee'
           closed syllables – as in 'hit'
o   open syllables – as in 'open'
           closed syllables – as in 'hot'
u   open syllables – like 'oo' in 'boot'
           closed syllables – as in 'put'

Dipthongs

ai   open syllables – like 'i' in kite: pantai
           (beach)
           closed syllables – pronounced as two
           separate sounds a – i
           baik (well/good) ba-eek
au   open syllables – like 'ow' in 'how'
           closed syllables – two separate sounds ow-
           u: laut (sea)

Stress Syllables generally carry equal stress, except
that in words of more than two syllables the
penultimate syllable is very slightly stressed.

Grammar At the basic level grammar is relatively simple: the article ('a' or 'the') is not expressed, verbs have no tenses and nouns remain the same for singular and plural. The plural form is indicated by repeating the noun.

rumah	=	house
rumah-rumah	=	houses

In normal speech, there is no need to repeat the noun when the context makes plurality clear.

Word order is as in English except that adjectives come after the noun: **bunga merah** – red flower

BASIC VOCABULARY AND EXPRESSIONS

GREETINGS

Good morning (up to 11am)	**Selamat pagi**
Good day (11am to 3pm)	**Selamat siang**
Good afternoon (3pm to sunset)	**Selamat sore**
Good evening/good night	**Selamat malam**

One may also be greeted with Halo and Hai (Hello and Hi), by the young and/or westernized.

Welcome	**Selamat datang**
How are you?	**Apa kabar?**
Well/fine.	**Baik.**
Fine, and how are you?	**Baik, dan apa kabar saudara?**
And you?	**Dan saudara?**
Fine, too.	**Baik juga.**

I must go now.	Saya harus pergi sekarang.
Goodbye (to person leaving)	Selamat jalan.
Goodbye (to person remaining remaining behind)	Selamat tinggal
See you later	Sampai jumpa lagi

POLITE PHRASES

Please	Tolong
Thankyou (very much)	Terima kasih (banyak)
Very good	Baik kesali
Please do	Silakan
You're welcome	Kembali
Excuse me/sorry/pardon	Maaf
It doesn't matter	Tidak apa
It's OK	Boleh
No/not	Tidak
Yes	Ya

PRONOUNS

I	Saya/Aku
You (singular)	Saudara
	kamu (familiar, do not use to adults)
	anda (becoming more frequent)
He/She	Dia
It	Ia
We	Kami (includes the person spoken to)
	Kita (excludes the person spoken to)

| You (plural) | Saudara sekalian |
| They | Mereka |

FORMS OF ADDRESS

Indonesians will address each other (and you) by titles of respect.

Bapak (or **Pak**) and **Ibu** (or **Bu**) are polite ways to address older men or women or officials.

Sir	**Tuan** (usually for foreigners)
Madam	**Nyonya**
Miss	**Nono**
Mr	**Pak, Tuan**
Mrs	**Bu, Nyonya**

A man who has made the pilgrimage to Mecca is addressed as **Haji**, a woman who has made the pilgrimage as **Hajjah**.

father	bapak/aya
mother	ibu
son	anak laki-laki
daughter	anak perempuan
parents	orang tua

USEFUL PHRASES

Where?	**Di mana?**
Where is the bank/post office?	**Di mana bank/kantor pos?**
Where are the toilets?	**Di mana WC?** (pronounced 'way say')

Ladies/Gents	Wanita/Laki-laki
Is/Are there?	Apa ada?
Is there a telephone?	Apa ada telepon?
Are there any toilets?	Apa ada WC?
Do you have any postcards?	Apa ada kertu pos?
	(In practice 'Apa' may be dropped – **Ada** kertu pos?
I would like/I want	Saya mau
I'd like a bottle of beer.	Saya mau sebotol
bir.	
How much?	Berapa?
How much does it cost?	Berapa harganya?
How much are the bananas a kilo?	Berapa harga pisang sekilo?
Thank you	Terima Kasih
good	bagus
do not	jangan

TIME

Today	Hari ini
Tomorrow	Besok
Yesterday	Kemarin
The day before yesterday	Kemarin dulu
The day after tomorrow	Lusa
Now	Sekarang
Later	Nanti
What time is it?	Jam berapa sekarang?

DAYS

Monday	Senin

Tuesday	**Selasa**
Wednesday	**Rabu**
Thursday	**Kamis**
Friday	**Jumat**
Saturday	**Sabtu**
Sunday	**Minggu**

NUMBERS

zero	nol
one	satu
two	dua
three	tiga
four	empat
five	lima
six	enam
seven	tujuh
eight	delapan
nine	sembilan
ten	sepuluh
eleven	sebelas
twelve	dua belas
thirteen	tiga belas
twenty	dua puluh
twenty-one	dua puluh satu
twenty-two	dua puluh dua
twenty-three	dua puluh tiga
thirty	tiga puluh

SIMPLE WANTS

to eat	makan
food	makanan
bread	roti

rice	beras
salt	garam
plate	piring
bowl	cawan
to drink	minum
drink	minuman
coffee	kopi
tea	teh
milk	susu
sugar	gula
cup	cankgir
beer	bir
glass	gelas
water	air
drinking water	air minum
cold	dingin
hot (temperature)	panas
hot (spicy)	pedas
large	besar
small	kecil
table	meja
chair	kursi
cigarette	rokok
bath	mandi
bathroom	tempat mandi
sleep	tidur
bed	tempat tidur
toilet	WC (way say)

Further Reading

There have been numerous books written about Indonesia, although most concern themselves with Java and Bali.

For Bali, the classic description of Balinese society and culture remains Miguel Covarrubias, *Island of Bali*, New York, Alfred A. Knopf, 1937; reprinted Kuala Lumpur, Oxford University Press, 1984.

Nigel Barley, *Not a Hazardous Sport*, London, Viking, 1988 is an entertaining account of Torajaland in Sulawesi.

Norman Lewis, *An Empire of the East. Travels in Indonesia*, London, Jonathan Cape, 1993 is a critical account of Indonesian rule in Sumatra, East Timor and Irian Jaya.

Brian May, *The Indonesian Tragedy*, Routledge & Kegan Paul, 1978, & in paperback by Graham Brash, Singapore the same year, is a history of Indonesia from independence which attempts to understand its problems and difficulties.

More general reading in handy and reasonably priced form may be found in two series produced by Oxford University Press in Singapore and Kuala Lumpur. The series Oxford in Asia Paperbacks, includes reprints of nineteenth and twentieth accounts of the region. The following are a few of the relevant titles:

Java

Jan Poortenaar, *An Artist in Java*; Augusta de Wit, *Java: Facts and Fancies*; E.R. Scidmore, *Java: The Gardens of the East*; James R. Russ, *Java: A Traveller's Anthology*; Jacques Dumarcay, *The Temples of Java* (he has also written on Borobudur); Michael Smythies, *Yogyakarta*.

Sumatra

F.M. Schnitger, *Forgotten Kingdoms in Sumatra*; Anthony Reid, *Witnesses to Sumatra*.

Bali

Miguel Covarrubias, Island of Bali; Hickman Powell, The Last Paradise; Adrian Vickers, Travelling in Bali.

Kalimantan

Carl Bock, The Head-Hunters of Borneo; William O. Krohn, In Borneo Jungles; Carl Lumholtz, Through Central Borneo.

General

Anna Forbes, Unbeaten Tracks in Islands of the Far East; George Miller, To the Spice Islands and Beyond; G.E.P. Collins, Makassar Sailing.

The series 'Images in Asia' includes the following titles: A.A.M.Djelantik, *Balinese paintings*; Derek Holmes & Stephen Nash, *The Birds of Java and Bali* and *The Birds of Sumatra and Kalimantan*; Sylvia Fraser-Lu, *Indonesian Batik: Processes, Patterns and Places*; Aart van Deek, *Life in the Javanese Kraton*. This series has general books on the arts of South-east Asia – musical instruments, the Malay kris, architecture, pottery and silver work – in which Indonesia also features.

For further information see:

Traveljakarta.com

Facts About Indonesia

Indonesia is the world's largest archipelago, incorporating over 13,000 islands and stretching 5,000 kilometres (3,200 miles) from the Southeast corner of the Asian continent to northern Australia.

It is a nation of great diversity and potential, which was created out of the territories of the Dutch East Indies in 1949. It occupies, as the islands always have, a region of great strategic importance, across the main east-west trade sea route between India and Europe on the one hand and China and Japan on the other.

Control of the Malacca and Sunda Straits and of the Pahlawan passage between Borneo and the southern Philippines enabled powerful and wealthy kingdoms to emerge. These sought to control the trade in regional products like spices, jungle products, beche-de-mere, pearls, and exotic items like hornbill, camphor, tortoise shell and edible birds nests, which were exchanged for the manufactures and trade goods of China, India and, later, Europe.

Modern Indonesia continues to occupy a strategic position between Asia and Australia and the Indian Ocean and Pacific. With a population of over 200 million it is the fifth most populous country in the world. It is an important member of ASEAN and has great economic potential not fully realized.

Some 70 per cent of Indonesia's population lives on Java, an island about the size of England. A policy of transmigration has not reduced the imbalance and has produced tensions on other islands. Moreover, the perception exists that the wealth produced by the less populous but resource-rich regions has not been effectively distributed back to them.

Climate

The climate is tropical with a wet and dry season, although in many regions the latter is better called a less wet season. Day temperatures at sea level rise to 26-30 degrees centigrade throughout the year and it is generally hot and humid. The evenings are pleasantly warm.

Jakarta is generally hotter and more uncomfortable than the other main cities.

Temperatures become cooler in the mountains. November to April is generally the rainy season and May to October is relatively dry.

This pattern is reversed in Sumatra and central Maluku. There are local variations caused by geographical factors.

Indonesia stretches across three time zones: Western, Central and Eastern Indonesian Standard Time (GMT + 7 hours to GMT + 9 hours).

Religion is important in everyday life. Islam is the religion of 80 per cent of the population. Indonesia thus has the world's largest Muslim population. There are substantial Buddhist, Hindu, Christian and Animist communities. Bali is predominantly Hindu. Belief in God is a tenet of the Panchasila or Five Principles.

Over 500 languages are spoken, but Bahasa Indonesia is the national language taught in schools and is spoken in all but the remotest areas. English is widely spoken in the main tourist areas.

The Indonesian economy remains in difficulties and there is widespread poverty. However, large areas of the country retain a largely rural subsistence economy based on agriculture, barter and the exchange of services. Western-style statistics can be misleading. On the whole, people are cheerful and display ingenuity in making do.

From the visitor's point of view Indonesia is a cheap place to visit, while an influx of visitors and tourists can only help the economy and the people in the present situation.

Business Hours

NB. The following times may vary from place to place. Be aware that government offices may be open but the officials you may have to deal with may not be available. It is advisable to visit the government offices early in the morning if you are to complete your business within the day.

Government offices are open from 8 am until 4 pm Monday to Friday, with a break for prayers between 11.30 am and 1.30 pm on Friday; and from 8 am until 2 pm on Saturday.

Post Offices follow government hours, though smaller ones may close at 2 pm.

Commercial offices and businesses are usually open from 8 am to 4 pm or from 9 am to 5 pm, with a variable lunch break of one hour. Some open on Saturday morning. Muslim businesses close between 11.30 am and 1.30 pm on Fridays.

Bank hours may vary slightly. Banks are usually open from 8 am to 3 pm Monday to Friday and from 8.30 am to 12 noon or 1 pm on Saturday.

Money lenders operate during normal shopping hours, which are variable.

Shopping centres in the cities open from 9 am to 8pm or 9 pm. Some also open on Sundays.

Smaller shops usually open early in the morning and remain open until late at night, but times may vary at the owner's whim.

Restaurants usually close at 11pm, but street stalls remain open until later.

A Note of Caution

Indonesia has experienced civil unrest in some areas, particularly in Aceh, Muluku, Lombok and Irian Jaya. Before deciding your itinerary, seek information on the current situation, but don't be deterred. Vast areas of the country remain open to you.

Currency

The Indonesian currency is the Rupiah (Rp.). All major currencies in travellers cheques and cash are exchangeable in banks and exchange offices. Credit cards are acceptable in larger hotels, businesses and restaurants and in tourist areas. In remoter areas you will need cash, much of it in in coins and small denomination notes as getting change is difficult.

Communications

Post and telephone services are generally good throughout the country. Most towns have post offices. International direct dialling is available in the cities and large towns and available from some hotels, though at a price. Look for the local telephone office (kantor telepon) or the more numerous but more expensive warpostel.

Index